I0441511

Affiliate Marketing Simplified Handbook For Beginners

A 10-Step Beginner's Guide To Achieving Financial Freedom Through Passive Income With Affiliate Marketing

Anais Sawayn

Table of Contents

CHAPTER ONE

Introduction

Affiliate marketing involves earning a commission by promoting and selling another person's or company's products. Affiliates find products they like, promote them, and earn a portion of the profits from each sale. This is tracked through special links between websites. Publishers earn commissions by endorsing products or services from retailers or advertisers through affiliate links. They receive payouts for specific actions, like generating sales, leads, clicks, or app downloads. Joining affiliate programs is often free, eliminating high startup expenses. With a successful strategy, affiliate marketing can evolve from a side gig to a lucrative online business, generating a substantial income.

How affiliate marketing works

Affiliate marketing entails recommending a product or service through channels like blogs, social media, podcasts, or websites. Affiliates earn commissions whenever someone buys using their unique affiliate link.

1. Display Store Z ad/link on your blog, website, or social platform.

2. Visitors click your special affiliate link.

3. Customers complete a purchase at Store Z.

4. The affiliate network logs the transaction.

5. Store Z confirms the purchase.

6. You receive a monetary commission. Commission rates vary, ranging from about 5% to as high as 50%, notably for class or

event promotions. Some programs offer a fixed rate per sale instead of a percentage.

Types of affiliate marketing

Affiliates often carry an air of uncertainty - it's hard to discern if they genuinely endorse a product or if it's purely for profit. Both scenarios persist today.

In 2009, renowned affiliate marketer Pat Flynn categorized affiliate marketers into three groups, shedding light on various online money-making methods within this sphere, regardless of moral inclinations.

The first type, "unattached" affiliate marketing, involves advertising products in a niche where you lack authority or connection with the customer. This approach often relies on pay-per-click ad campaigns with the hope that clicks lead to purchases, earning you a commission.

The allure of unattached affiliate marketing lies in its simplicity - no extensive groundwork is necessary. While successful affiliate marketing thrives on trust and reputation, some marketers prefer this method due to time constraints or a lack of interest in fostering relationships.

Elise Dopson, the founder of Sprocker Lovers, remarks, "Unattached affiliate marketing isn't a genuine business model; it's for those solely aiming for income generation. At Sprocker Lovers, our emphasis lies in community building and providing niche-specific education, like our focus on the sprocker spaniel dog breed, with sales as a secondary priority."

Related affiliate marketing

Affiliate marketing in a related niche involves endorsing products and services relevant to your field, even if you don't personally use them. Marketers in this category possess an audience, be it through blogging, YouTube, TikTok, or other platforms, and wield influence, becoming reliable sources for product recommendations despite lacking firsthand experience.

While this approach can amplify affiliate earnings, it poses the risk of promoting untested offerings. There's a chance of endorsing an inferior product or service, unbeknownst to you. A single misguided endorsement can erode the trust painstakingly built with your audience. Trust and transparency are fundamental; without them, establishing a sustainable affiliate marketing venture becomes challenging.

Involved affiliate marketing

Engaged affiliate marketing revolves around endorsing products and services that the marketer has genuinely used and believes in. According to Elise, "Engaged affiliate marketing is the way forward. It's founded on trust and authenticity, benefiting both your audience and business."

In this method, the affiliate leverages their influence to recommend products and services that their followers might truly find valuable, steering away from simply paying for clicks on banner ads. Establishing this level of credibility with an audience demands time but is vital for fostering a sustainable business.

Elise highlights that the engaged approach simplifies advertising for affiliate partners. "No need to rely on costly PPC ads and hope for clicks and sales. A genuine Instagram Story or blog post sharing your experience with a product goes a long way." Elise prefers this method because of its honesty, emphasizing that it's "the sole authentic path to becoming a trusted authority in any field."

CHAPTER TWO

Pros In Affiliate Marketing

Affiliate marketing holds significant worth due to its burgeoning popularity. Statista forecasts the industry to surge to $8.2 billion by 2022 from $5.4 billion in 2017. Moreover, it's a business venture with minimal to no costs, offering substantial profit potential. But, before immersing yourself, it's crucial to weigh the pros and cons of venturing into affiliate marketing.

While the industry's growth is promising, entrepreneurs opt for this referral marketing path for several other reasons.

Ease of Execution

Your role primarily involves managing the digital marketing facets of product building and sales. This means you sidestep the more demanding tasks like development, support, or order fulfillment.

Low Risk

Affiliate programs typically have no entry fees, allowing you to start earning from established products or services without initial investments. Moreover, affiliate marketing can yield passive income through commissions—an optimal income stream. Although it requires upfront effort to create traffic sources, your affiliate lnk can continually generate income.

Scalability

Successful affiliate marketing presents opportunities to significantly boost earnings without additional staffing. Introducing new products to your existing audience and crafting campaigns for additional offerings can expand your revenue while your earlier efforts continue generating income.

However, it's vital to recognize that exceptional affiliate marketing hinges on trust. Despite the array of products available for promotion, it's advisable to spotlight only those you personally use or endorse. Even when a product aligns with your interests or hobbies, excelling as an affiliate marketer demands substantial effort and dedication.

Cons

Affiliate marketing comes with its share of drawbacks when compared to other marketing methods. Before diving in, let's explore the challenges you might encounter on your journey to success in affiliate marketing.

Requires Patience

Unlike a get-rich-quick scheme, affiliate marketing demands time and perseverance to build an audience and wield influence. Experimentation with different channels, researching credible products, blogging, social media engagement, hosting virtual events, and other lead-generating activities are essential for success.

Commission-Based

As an affiliate marketer, you won't receive a fixed paycheck. Compensation relies on commissions, be it for leads, clicks, or sales. Tracking individuals' actions through temporary browser cookies determines your payout.

Limited Control Over Programs

Affiliates must adhere to the rules set by the companies they work with, following specific guidelines for product or service presentation. Competitors also comply with these standards, demanding creativity to stand out.

CHAPTER THREE

How Affiliate Marketers Earn

Affiliate income varies significantly, ranging from a few hundred dollars monthly to six-figure annual earnings. Greater following often translates to higher earnings, with an average annual salary for affiliate marketers surpassing $53,000 according to Payscale.

Successful affiliate marketer Ryan Robinson generates over $17,000 monthly solely through affiliate income. Payment models in affiliate programs vary, determining the goals for which you get paid. These models include:

Pay Per Sale: Common for e-commerce, earning you a commission for each sale.

Pay Per Action: Pays for specific actions like sign-ups, clicks, contact requests, etc.

Pay Per Install: Rewards for generating software or app installations from your traffic.

Pay Per Lead: Payment for each sign-up, commonly used for lead generation.

Pay Per Click: Rare, earning commission for each click on your affiliate link, mostly for brand awareness.

Earnings largely depend on the affiliate niche. For instance, business-related programs offer an average commission rate of $70.99, while book and clothing categories yield around $6 per commission. The maximum average commission observed stands at approximately $289.06 per sale.

Seller and product creators

The individual or entity selling a product, whether an independent entrepreneur or a corporation, is termed the vendor, merchant, product creator, or retailer. Their offering can range from physical items like household goods to services such as makeup tutorials.

Referred to as the brand, the seller isn't obligated to actively engage in marketing efforts but may also serve as the advertiser, benefiting from revenue sharing within the realm of affiliate marketing.

For instance, the seller might be an e-commerce merchant venturing into drop-shipping, aiming to access a new audience by compensating affiliate sites for promoting their products. Alternatively, the seller could represent a SAAS company employing affiliates to market their marketing software.

The affiliate or publisher

Referred to as a publisher, the affiliate can be an individual or a company entrusted with marketing the seller's product in an enticing manner to potential consumers. Essentially, the affiliate's role involves promoting the product to demonstrate its value or benefits, persuading consumers to make a purchase. Upon the consumer's purchase, the affiliate earns a share of the generated revenue.

Affiliates frequently target a precise audience, aligning with their interests. This approach establishes a distinct niche or personal brand for the affiliate, drawing in consumers more likely to engage with the promotions.

The consumer

For the affiliate system to function, sales are crucial, and these sales are initiated by the consumer or customer.

The affiliate endeavors to market the product or service to consumers via various channels such as social media, blogs, or YouTube videos. If the consumer perceives the product as valuable or beneficial, they can follow the affiliate link and proceed to check out on the merchant's website. Upon the customer's purchase, the affiliate earns a share of the generated revenue.

However, it's essential for the customer to be aware that you, as the affiliate, receive a commission from the product sale. As per the Federal Trade Commission's guidelines, an affiliate marketer must transparently disclose their association with the retailer. This disclosure empowers consumers to assess the weight of your endorsement.

A clear disclaimer like "The products I'm featuring in this video were provided by Company X" furnishes viewers with the necessary information, allowing them to make informed decisions regarding the purchase of the affiliate product.

CHAPTER FOUR

How Much You Can Earn

The affiliate marketing sector exhibits steady growth. Statista projected that spending on affiliate marketing in the U.S. would soar to $8.2 billion by 2022, a significant leap from $5.4 billion in 2017 and $1.6 billion in 2010.

Another study by VigLink delves deeper into the earnings of affiliate marketers. The survey revealed that 9% of publishers generated over $50,000 in affiliate income in 2016. A majority of merchants, accounting for 65%, reported earning between 5% and 20%

of their annual revenue from affiliate marketing. Experience also played a role in revenue generation, with 60% of the highest-earning merchants having engaged in affiliate marketing for five years or longer.

65%

The majority of merchants mentioned that they derived between 5% and 20% of their annual revenue from affiliate marketing.

The primary advantage of affiliate marketing is its potential for generating revenue on autopilot once established, requiring a consistent flow of traffic to your blog or website. Nevertheless, there are drawbacks to consider.

Changes in a company's affiliate program terms can directly impact your earnings. Associating with unsuitable businesses may hinder your income if your audience isn't inclined to purchase their products or services. With the expanding landscape of affiliate marketing, expect intense competition from other marketers endorsing the same products.

Sustaining visitor engagement demands a continuous influx of fresh content on your website.

Developing A Successful Affiliate Marketing Strategy

Entering affiliate marketing might seem straightforward, but establishing sustainable income from affiliate programs requires a different approach. Before diving in, laying a solid foundation is crucial.

Begin by understanding your audience's preferences: What goods and services resonate with them? Identify products you currently use and genuinely endorse to recommend to your audience. While adding affiliate program links to your site is an option, focus on products relevant to your website's theme to enhance click-through rates and retain your audience.

Conduct thorough research on individual affiliate programs, comparing their structures, commission rates, and payment frequencies. Comprehend any regulations imposed by affiliate networks. Aligning your affiliate marketing content with your niche can generally yield better returns.

Maintain transparency with your readers by including a disclosure in your blog posts or website, informing them about potential affiliate links. This not only enhances your credibility but also complies with the Federal Trade Commission's endorsement guidelines.

The Conclusion

Affiliate marketing holds the potential for substantial earnings, yet transforming it into a genuine business requires dedicated time and financial investment. Before venturing into affiliate marketing, thorough research is essential.

Additionally, avoid relying solely on affiliate marketing. Diversifying income streams is prudent when aiming to establish a profitable website. Supplementing with traditional advertisements or selling your own products can serve as viable alternatives should your affiliate marketing revenue decline.

THE END